THE LIFE OF CHARLEMAGNE

Ninth-century equestrian bronze statuette reputedly of Charlemagne
but possibly Charles the Bald. The horse is fifteenth century

EINHARD THE FRANK

THE LIFE OF
CHARLEMAGNE

Translated and with an Introduction by
LEWIS THORPE

LONDON
THE FOLIO SOCIETY
MCMLXX

PRINTED IN GREAT BRITAIN

Printed and bound by Jarrold & Sons Ltd, Norwich
Set in Poliphilus 12 point leaded 1 point

CONTENTS

INTRODUCTION

THE LIFE OF CHARLEMAGNE

The coronation of Charlemagne. Charlemagne enthroned

ILLUSTRATIONS

INTRODUCTION

CHARLEMAGNE, KING AND EMPEROR

The military campaigns

Charlemagne was born *c*. 742 as the eldest son of Pepin the Short and his wife Bertrada. He had a younger brother, Carloman, who was born *c*. 751, and a third brother, Pepin, died as a child. There was also a sister, Gisela, born in 757. Pepin the Short was Mayor of the Palace under Childeric III, the last of the Merovingian kings, until, on 28 July 754, Pope Stephen II crowned him King of the Franks and appointed his two sons Charlemagne and Carloman as his joint heirs. After his coronation King Pepin the Short lived for a further fourteen years and, immediately before his death at Saint-Denis on 24 September 768, he divided his lands between his two sons. In terms of modern countries they included much of Germany, most of Holland, the whole of Belgium and Switzerland, and almost the whole of France. The centre and south of this vast area was given to Carloman. To Charlemagne was apportioned a great half-circle running westwards from Ratisbon on the Danube and from the River Saal to the North Sea, and then southwards to the Pyrenees.

The disparity of personality and experience between the two brothers at the moment of their succession was very great. Charlemagne was about twenty-six and, although he had never held great authority, he had been associated with his father in most of the events of the last few years of his life. Carloman was a boy of about seventeen. Both born of the same parents, Charlemagne is supposed to have been a love-child while Carloman was legitimate. As we see him through the accounts of later writers who were for the most part his dependants, Charlemagne was a man of limitless energy, great resolution and considerable personal strength; Carloman, seen through the prejudiced eyes of these same writers, appears to have been peevish, given to self-pity and the easy victim of the flatterers who surrounded him.

The period immediately following 768 was largely occupied by problems which the two young kings, and Charlemagne in particular, had inherited from their father, but to these Charlemagne added a domestic complication of his own and his mother's making. During the last years of the reign of King Pepin, Aquitaine had been in revolt and, in 769, a certain Hunold led a new rising of the Aquitanians of the south-west in Saintonge and Poitou. Charle-magne moved with his army towards the southern reaches of his inheritance, met his brother Carloman at Moncontour and was refused assistance by him. The revolt of the Aquitanians was put down, but Charlemagne never saw his brother again. With the help of their mother Bertrada, relations were patched up between them, for an open quarrel would have been of no advantage to either of the Frankish kings. Then, to what must have been the considerable relief of Charlemagne, Carloman died suddenly in December 771. His vassals immediately did homage to Charlemagne and the entire territory of Pepin the Short was thus united once more under one ruler. Charlemagne then turned to face new difficulties in the east. In 770, at the persuasion of his mother and to the great annoyance of Pope Stephen III, he had married the daughter of Desiderius, King of the Longobards; a year later he dismissed his young wife and in her place married the Swabian Hildigard; on the death of Carloman in 771, that king's widow Gerberga and her young sons joined Charlemagne's repudiated wife at the court of this same Desiderius in Pavia; after a brief period of alliance with Rome, Desiderius quarrelled with Pope Stephen III; and to aggravate all these circum-stances, which were difficult enough for Charlemagne in all conscience, Desiderius saw a deadly threat to his own Longobard kingdom in the junction of the dead Carloman's territories with those of his formidable brother. Charlemagne assembled his forces at Geneva, crossed the Alps and, in October 773, began to besiege Pavia, the capital of Desiderius and his Longobard kingdom. The city fell in June 774, Desiderius was deposed and Charlemagne added a new territory to those which he already possessed.

With the revolt in Aquitaine crushed, Carloman dead and his lands engulfed, Desiderius beaten and his Longobard kingdom captured, and with relations established on a firm footing with the Papacy, Charlemagne had already turned to face a long series of most bloodthirsty wars with the Saxons in the north. These were to continue intermittently from 772 until 804, for a period of more than thirty years. Only in 804 was Saxonia finally conquered and pacified.

During this long period of the Saxon wars Charlemagne had many military preoccupations elsewhere. In 775–6 Rotgaud, the Longobard Duke of Friuli, aggravated beyond endurance by the territorial claims of Charlemagne's ally, Pope Hadrian I, revolted but was killed in battle. In 778 Charlemagne crossed the Pyrenees into Spain, penetrated as far south as Saragossa, which he failed to take, destroyed the walls of Pamplona and, as he moved back into Aquitania, suffered the defeat to his rearguard known as the battle of Roncevaux. Duke Tassilo III of Bavaria, who had been in revolt against Pepin the Short years before and whose wife Liutberga was one of the daughters of Desiderius, the deposed King of the Longo-bards, conspired with his brother-in-law, Areghis, but was finally forced to surrender and, in 788, like Desiderius before him, was sent to a monastery. As Charlemagne and his armies forced their way ever deeper into the lands of the Saxons, they gradually began to join battle with peoples who lived even farther to the east, the Abodrites, the Wiltzes, the Sorbs, the Avars, the Wends and, more to the south, the Slavs. In the west the Carolingian leader Audulf won a victory against the Bretons in 786, as did Wido in 799, and a year later the Breton leaders met at Tours and offered their allegiance to Charlemagne; but by 811 they were in revolt once more. In the north Godefrid, King of the Northmen, who had watched the successive reduction of the Saxons and the Abodrites, and then the fighting with the Wiltzes, built an immense earthen rampart called the Danework south of the River Eider, from the Baltic to the North Sea. In 808 he mounted a campaign against the Franks, and in 810 he sent a huge fleet to ravage the Frisian Islands. Charlemagne, who was then nearly seventy, marched northwards to meet Godefrid at Verden, but before the two forces could join battle the Danish leader was murdered. It was Charlemagne's last expedition.

Diplomacy and administration
In the midst of all this military activity, and largely because of it, Charlemagne was at the same time engaged in diplomatic relations with the rulers of many other lands. Irene, joint ruler of the Empire in Constantinople, in 781 proposed a marriage between her infant son, the Emperor Constantine VI, and Charlemagne's daughter Rotrude, but this was eventually broken off six years later. From 789 to 796 Charlemagne was in correspondence with Offa, King of

Mercia; and Eardulf, King of Northumbria, visited him as a fugitive in Nimeguen in 808. His relations with Harun-al-Rachid are mentioned in some detail by Einhard: he sent envoys to Bagdad in 797 and 807, and messengers from Harun arrived at Ivrea in 801 and Aachen in 807. In 803 the Emperor Nicephorus I, who had succeeded the Empress Irene in the previous year, sent an embassy to Charlemagne. In the course of the single year 810 Charlemagne concluded peace treaties with Nicephorus I, with El Hakem the Cruel, Emir of Cordova, and with Hemming, King of the Danes, who had succeeded to his father Godefrid.

Four times Charlemagne visited Rome: in 774, during the siege of Pavia, when he was welcomed by Pope Hadrian I; in 781, when Hadrian crowned the two young princes, Pepin and Lewis, as Kings of the Longobards and the Aquitanians; in 787, when Charlemagne spent Easter with the Pope; and in 800 when, on Christmas Day, Pope Leo III crowned Charlemagne as Emperor.

All this activity, both military and civil, spread over territories so extensive in days when travelling was so difficult, demanded a complicated administrative machine at the centre, if it was to be successful. In the years following his coronation Charlemagne devoted his attention largely to administrative problems. Each year saw new additions to the code of laws contained in the corpus of capitularies. Most of the reforms concerned the administration of justice; but at the same time the military system was changed radically. Charlemagne could not afford a standing army: but now the obligation of periodic military service was moved from the individual to the land held. The production of a suitably armed soldier for a specified period was henceforth the responsibility of the holder or holders, few or numerous, of a given piece of land, who chose, paid and equipped their nominee. New edicts were announced to provincial assemblies by Charlemagne's *missi dominici*, or royal commissioners, pairs of unpaid emissaries, of high rank, one a churchman, one a layman, sent out on circuit to a given neighbourhood. Failure to observe the edicts was tried by local law-courts, consisting of seven *scabini* or jurymen, elected for life; and the equity of the decisions of the *scabini* was supervised by the local count. In 802 Charlemagne reduced to writing the various national codes. All of this must have seemed much better to the court official writing it down on parchment than it did to the individual inhabitant of some far-flung

township in the Carolingian Empire. The laws were often inequit-
able and unjust; the *scabini* did not understand the laws and were in
any case, afraid of the local court; the *missi* were busy men, who had
heavy commitments and responsibilities at home and could ill afford
these long excursions on circuit; the provincial assemblies listened to
the new edicts, signified their assent without too much effort of
comprehension, and then, on the departure of the *missi*, continued
to act exactly as they had always acted before; so many men of talent
were needed at the centre to set out and promulgate the laws that
there were too few men of talent left on the periphery to see that they
were observed; and those who planned the laws were often out of
touch with reality.

The Carolingian Renaissance

Charlemagne himself was illiterate: Einhard describes his rather
pathetic attempts to learn to write, but concludes that, 'although he
tried very hard, he had begun too late in life and he made little
progress'. His own language was Frankish; he spoke Latin well and
understood some Greek. He learned the elements of grammar from
Peter the Deacon, and Alcuin taught him rhetoric, dialectic, mathematics and astrology. His respect for learning and the liberal arts
seems to have been genuine and deep-rooted. Gradually, as the years
passed, Charlemagne assembled at his court in Aachen many of the
most learned men of Europe. In 781 he met again in Parma the
Englishman Alcuin, who had previously visited his court. From 782
to 796 Alcuin was at Aachen, and from then until his death in 804
he lived in his abbey of Saint-Martin in Tours. Some time before the
conquest of the Longobard kingdom in 785, Charlemagne had
come into contact with Paul the Deacon, Peter of Pisa and Paulinus,
later of Aquileia. Einhard, a Frank born in the Maingau, moved to
the Palace School in Aachen in 791. These men, and others like
them, were the mainsprings of the Carolingian Renaissance. During
his years at Aachen, Alcuin organized the Palace School. Under
him the school became an important factor in national life; it
developed into a well-defined and highly favoured institution. Any
magnate might send his sons, nor were humble antecedents allowed
to exclude a boy of talent. Plebeian or patrician, it mattered nothing
to Charlemagne: he singled out the most proficient with rare impar-
tiality and promoted them to vacant offices or preferments. Alcuin

taught in person and enlisted all the other literati in the service. The King set the fashion of taking lessons, and all his family were put to school. Being a court affair, the school accompanied the royal household in its wanderings. It was not hampered by elaborate paraphernalia. Alcuin sent envoys far and wide to purchase books for his pupils, but the library which he gathered must have been both small and portable. The primers of the elementary subjects – orthography, grammar, rhetoric and dialectic – written by himself, are still extant and are printed in his works. Theology was seen as the centre of all learning. Students who had shown marked ability were sent out to become the abbots of Frankish monasteries. Great monastic schools were developed at Fulda and Tours, and later at Corbie, Saint-Wandrille, Saint-Gall and elsewhere. Latin was restored as a literary language, spelling was revised and penmanship remodelled on the old uncial letters. The works of the great writers of ancient Rome were preserved in the Carolingian copying-schools. Einhard tells us that Charlemagne also ordered the old sagas of the Frankish peoples to be written out, and that he began a grammar of his native tongue.

Einhard's life contains references to the thermal baths at Aachen, the cathedral modelled on San Vitale in Ravenna, the Imperial palace and the great bridge constructed over the River Rhine at Mainz. These show yet another side of Charlemagne's immense creative ability.

EINHARD THE FRANK

We possess a considerable amount of information about Einhard, the author of the *Vita Caroli* or the *Life of Charlemagne*. In his introduction he tells us that Charlemagne was his master and patron, and that he had seen with his own eyes the happenings which he describes. His two immediate reasons for writing were the personal knowledge which he possessed of Charlemagne, and the debt of gratitude which he owed to this remarkable king and emperor, who had helped him to continue his education and with whom he had long lived on friendly terms.

In his reticence Einhard does not even name himself. This is remedied by a prologue written for the *Life of Charlemagne* by Walahfrid Strabo, Abbot of Reichenau, and by information provided

The coronation of Charlemagne as Emperor by Pope Leo III

by other ninth-century writers who knew Einhard personally. A man of comparatively noble birth, he was born in the Maingau. His parents were called Einhart and Engilfrit, and during the abbacy of Baugolf (779–802) he was sent to be educated in the monastery of Fulda, in Hesse, some sixty miles north-east of Frankfurt, of which institution his father and mother were benefactors. Soon after 791 he was sent by Abbot Baugolf to the Palace School of Charlemagne at Aachen. By his intelligence, wisdom and probity, virtues which are rarely found united in the same man at any period in history, he soon made his mark at court, and he became the adviser and personal friend of Charlemagne. He seems to have been a man of many talents. In one of his letters to Charlemagne, Alcuin calls Einhard by the nickname Bezaleel, which the Emperor apparently used for him. This nickname is repeated by Walahfrid Strabo in a poem written in 829, long after the death of Charlemagne. Alcuin himself had been given the name Flaccus and the two scholars and their friends addressed Charlemagne as David. If the name Bezaleel is to be taken at all seriously, it may imply that Einhard was skilled in metal-work, wood-carving and the cutting of gems.

After the death of Charlemagne in 814, Einhard remained in high favour with his successor, Lewis the Pious, a fact which clearly astonished Walahfrid Strabo. It was at this period that he seems to have married Imma, the sister of Bernhard, Bishop of Worms and Abbot of Weissenburg. His married state did not prevent Lewis from making him abbot of a long series of monasteries. In 815 he was given a grant of lands at Michlinstat and at Mulinheim, later to be known as Seligenstadt, 'the city of the Saints', from the church which Einhard built there and the relics of Saint Marcellinus and Saint Peter which he had carried there. Gradually as the years passed his health began to fail. In letters dated 829 and 830 he wrote of pains in his stomach and his back, and in this latter year he left Aachen and went to live in Seligenstadt. Imma died in 836. The death of Einhard himself occurred on 14 March 840.

THE VITA CAROLI OF EINHARD

There are in existence four works written by Einhard, all of them in Latin: the *Vita Caroli*, of which a new translation is printed in this book; a series of seventy-one letters, called the *Einharti Epistolae*, which, as far as they can be dated, run from 814 to 840; the *De translatione et miraculis sanctorum suorum Marcellini et Petri*; and a book dedicated to Servatus Lupus, the *Libellus de adoranda Cruce*.

It is thought that the *Life of Charlemagne* was written between 829 and 836, for it is first mentioned by this same Servatus Lupus, later Abbot of Ferrières (840–62), in a letter which he wrote at some unspecified moment between these two dates. This means, in all probability, that Einhard composed it after he had left Aachen and when he was living in comparative peace in Seligenstadt.

Four things immediately strike one about the *Life of Charlemagne*: it is occasionally inaccurate in its data, and, in a number of ways, it seems deliberately to obscure the truth, always in favour of the Emperor; the author never addresses us in person, except in the introduction; in view of the remarkable series of events which Einhard has to recount for us, his biography is extremely short; and, when viewed as a work of art, especially by those accustomed to considering the great masterpieces of European literature, in their correct sequence, over the last two thousand years, there is a strange perfection about it which becomes all the more unexpected when we remember that it was written in Seligenstadt in the 830s.

The brevity of the *Life of Charlemagne*, the clarity and the general excellence of Einhard's Latin style compared with that of the other German Latinists of the time and the neat and satisfying way in which his biography is set out all bring us to a new consideration. R. B. Mowat wrote of Einhard's 'genuine literary talent'. Louis Halphen has been equally admiring. The truth is that Einhard was following a model, or rather a series of twelve models. It is known that a manuscript of the *De vita Caesarum* of Suetonius existed in the library of the monastery of Fulda at the time when Einhard studied there. He had clearly read this work with great attention and his *Vita Caroli* follows so closely the life of Augustus in particular, both in form and in wording, that he may well have had a transcription with him when he was writing his own work at Seligenstadt, unless, as is possible, he knew much of Suetonius by heart. To say that Einhard is following his models so faithfully and with such slavish imitation that the *Life of Charlemagne* is virtually a thirteenth chapter added to the twelve which Suetonius left to us is perhaps an over‑statement, but in length, shape, sequence of material and even in expression there is undoubtedly a most striking similarity. This in part explains the literary excellence of the *Life of Charlemagne*. It also explains certain weaknesses. We might have hoped for something longer, but each of the twelve lives written by Suetonius was one chapter only in a book. In each of his *Lives* Suetonius follows a fixed pattern, and Einhard has thought it necessary to arrange his material in the same rigid way. Finally, in his portrayal of Charlemagne's character and personal habits, Einhard painted a picture which is false in that it resembles so closely those of the twelve Caesars.

The *Life of Charlemagne* has been called 'the most striking result of the Classical Renaissance so diligently fostered at the court of Charlemagne by the Emperor himself' and French critics have maintained that as a biography there is nothing to compare with it between the works of Suetonius himself and *Le livre des saintes paroles et des bonnes actions de Saint Louis* by Joinville.

THE LIFE OF CHARLEMAGNE

Ty endroit parle qui ciz fu qui la gieste
descript et la maniere de viure des roys ·J·
Il dit donques egintaux
chapellain et notiry ou
palays le victorien prin
ce et le tres renomme
empeire charlemaine
jay propose adscaure ses
meurs et sa vie alayde
de nostre seigneur au

Archbishop Turpin and Einhard

WALAHFRID STRABO'S PROLOGUE

It is generally accepted that it was Einhard who wrote this life of the most glorious Emperor Charlemagne, together with the description of the historical events which form the background to the life. Einhard was one of the most highly thought of among all the palace officials of that time, not only for his knowledge of what really took place but also for his personal character, which was beyond reproach. He himself played a part in almost all the events which he described, so that he was really able to bring the strictest accuracy to his testimony.

Einhard was born in the eastern part of the Frankish dominions, in the district which is called the Maingau. As a boy he received his earliest education in the monastery of Fulda, in the school founded by Saint Boniface himself. It was Baugolf, the abbot of the monastery of Fulda,* who sent Einhard from there to the palace of Charlemagne. The reason for this was not Einhard's noble birth, although, indeed, he came from a distinguished family; it was because his talents and intelligence were most remarkable and that, even at so young an age, he gave great promise of the wisdom which was later to make him so famous. Of all kings Charlemagne was the most eager in his search for wise men and in his determination to provide them with living conditions in which they could pursue knowledge in all reasonable comfort. In this way Charlemagne was able to offer to the cultureless and, I might say, almost completely unenlightened territory of the realm which God had entrusted to him, a new enthusiasm for all human knowledge. In its earlier state of barbarousness, his kingdom had been hardly touched at all by any such zeal, but now it opened its eyes to God's illumination. In our own time the thirst for knowledge is disappearing again: the light of wisdom is less and less sought after and is now becoming rare again in most men's minds.

This tiny man, then – for Einhard's lack of inches was a great handicap to him – by reason of his wisdom and probity, achieved

* Baugolf was abbot from 779 to 802.

such fame at the court of Charlemagne, who was himself a greater seeker after knowledge, that among all the ministers of his royal Majesty there was hardly anyone to be found with whom the most mighty and sagacious King of his time was prepared to discuss more freely the secrets of his private affairs. There is no doubt at all that Einhard deserved this distinction: for not only in the time of Charlemagne himself, but under the Emperor Lewis the Pious, too – and this indeed is a miracle – when the Frankish state was shaken by innumerable troubles of all sorts and was falling to pieces in many areas, with God to watch over him and with a certain sense of direction in his personal conduct which can only have been divinely inspired, he preserved this reputation for brilliance which laid him open to the malice and ill-will of other men. What is more, he suffered no irremediable harm because of it.

All this I say so that nobody may have doubts about what Einhard has written, simply for want of knowing the man, the great debt of praise which he owed to the memory of his patron and the scrupulousness of the truth which he offered to the inquiring reader.

I, Walahfrid Strabo, have inscribed the headings* in this little work and made the chapter divisions as it seemed best to me, so that the reader may more easily consult any particular point in which he is interested.

---

* These rubrics are not included in editions of the text.

EINHARD'S INTRODUCTION

Having once made up my mind to describe the life and the day-to-day habits of Charlemagne, my lord and patron, and to write the public history of this most distinguished and deservedly most famous king, I have determined to be as succinct as possible. My aim has been to omit nothing relevant which has come to my notice and yet to avoid insulting the intelligence of fastidious readers by explaining at great length every fresh item of information. In this way my book may please even those who scorn the tales of antiquity as set down by the most competent and eloquent of historians.

I am sure that there are many men of leisure and learning who feel that the history of this present age should not be neglected and that the many events which are happening in our own lifetime should not be held unworthy of record and be permitted to sink into silence and oblivion. On the contrary, these men are so filled with a desire for immortality that they prefer, I know, to set out the noble deeds of their contemporaries in writings which may well have no great merit, rather than permit their own name and reputation to disappear from the memory of future generations by writing nothing at all. However that may be, I have decided that I myself should not refuse to write a book of this kind, for I am very conscious of the fact that no one can describe these events more accurately than I, for I was present when they took place and, as they say, I saw them with my own eyes. What is more, I cannot be absolutely sure that these happenings will in fact ever be described by anyone else. I have therefore decided that it would be better to record these events myself for the information of posterity, even though there is a chance that they may be repeated in other histories, rather than allow the extraordinary life of this most remarkable king, the greatest man of all those living in his own period, to sink into the shades of oblivion, together with his outstanding achievements, which can scarcely be matched by modern men.

Another reason had occurred to me and this, I think, not an irrational one. Even by itself it would have been sufficient to compel me to write what follows. I mean the care which Charlemagne took in my upbringing, and the friendly relations which I enjoyed with him and his children from the moment when I first began to live at his court.* By this friendship he bound me to him and made me his debtor both in life and in death. I should indeed seem ungrateful, and could rightly be condemned as such, if I so far forgot the benefits he conferred upon me as to pass over in silence the outstanding and most remarkable deeds of a man who was so kind to me, suffering him to remain unchronicled and unpraised, just as if he had never lived.

My own meagre talent, small and insignificant, non-existent almost, is not equal to writing this life and setting it out in full. What was needed was the literary skill of a Cicero.

Here then you have a book which perpetuates the memory of the greatest and most distinguished of men. There is nothing to marvel at in it beyond Charlemagne's own deeds, except perhaps the fact that I, not a Roman by birth and a man but little versed in the tongue of the Romans, should have imagined that I could compose any-thing acceptable and suitable in the Latin language, and that I should have pushed my impudence so far as to scorn the advice given by Cicero in Book I of the *Tusculanae Disputationes*. Speaking about Latin authors, he says there, as you can read for yourself: 'For a man to commit his thoughts to writing when he can neither arrange them nor bring any new light to bear upon them, and, indeed, when he has no attraction whatsoever to offer to his reader, is a senseless waste of time, and of paper, too.' This distinguished orator's advice would certainly have deterred me from writing, had I not made up my mind to risk being condemned by other men and endanger my own small reputation by setting these matters down, rather than preserve my reputation at the expense of the memory of so famous a man.

* In his early days at Aachen Einhard received instruction in the company of Charlemagne's sons and it was at this period that he began his friendship with Lewis the Pious.

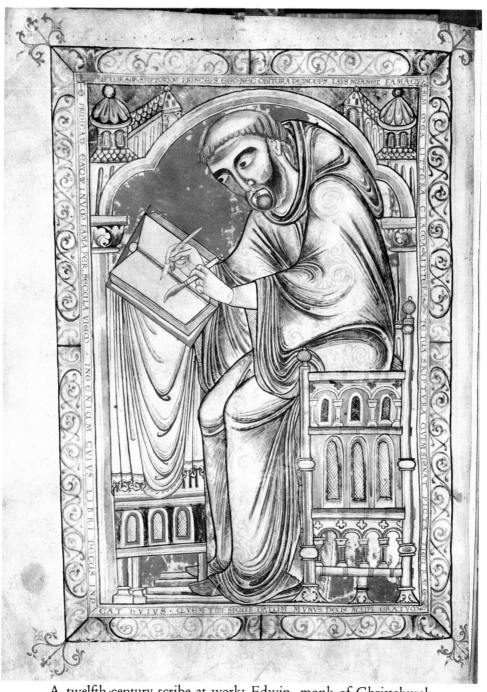

A twelfth-century scribe at work: Edwin, monk of Christchurch, Canterbury

BOOK I

THE EARLY CAROLINGIANS

The Merovingian dynasty, from which the Franks were accustomed to choose their Kings, is thought to have lasted down to King Childeric III, who was deposed on the order of Stephen II, the Pope of Rome.* His hair was cut short and he was shut up in a monastery. Though this dynasty may seem to have come to an end only with Childeric III, it had really lost all power years before and it no longer possessed anything at all of importance beyond the empty title of King. The wealth and the power of the kingdom were held tight in the hands of certain leading officials of the court, who were called the Mayors of the Palace, and on them supreme authority devolved. All that was left to the King was that, content with his royal title, he should sit on the throne, with his hair long and his beard flowing, and act the part of a ruler, giving audience to the ambassadors who arrived from foreign parts and then, when their time of departure came, charging them with answers which seemed to be of his own devising but in which he had in reality been coached or even directed. Beyond this empty title of King, and a precarious living wage which the Mayor of the Palace allowed him at his own discretion, the King possessed nothing at all of his own, except a single estate with an extremely small revenue, in which he had his dwelling and from which came the servants, few enough in number, who ministered to his wants and did him honour. Whenever he needed to travel, he went in a cart which was drawn in country style by yoked oxen, with a cowherd to drive them.† In this fashion he would go to the palace and to the general assembly of his people, which was held each year to settle the affairs of the kingdom, and in this fashion he would return home again. It was the Mayor of

* It was Pope Zacharias who was consulted about the deposition of Childeric III. Pope Stephen II crowned Pepin the Short at Saint Denis in 754.

† This cart, like the long hair and beards of the Merovingian kings, was really a sign of their royal and religious dignity.

the Palace who took responsibility for the administration of the realm
and all matters which had to be done or planned at home or abroad.

At the time of Childeric III's deposition, Pepin the Short, the
father of Charlemagne, was already performing this duty as if by
hereditary right. Charles Martel, the father of Pepin the Short, had
performed the same office with great success, inheriting it in his turn
from his own father, Pepin of Herstal. It was Charles Martel who
had crushed the despots who were claiming dominion for themselves
throughout the whole land of the Franks. It was he, too, who had
conquered the Saracens, when they were striving to occupy Gaul, in
two battles, one in Aquitaine, near the city of Poitiers [732], and the
other by the River Berre, near Narbonne [737]. In this way he
compelled them to withdraw into Spain.

It was customary for this title of Mayor of the Palace to be granted
by the people only to those who outshone all others by family
distinction and the extent of their wealth.

Pepin the Short, the father of Charlemagne, held the office for
some years, under, if that is the word, King Childeric III, about
whom I have told you. It had been handed down to him and his
brother Carloman by their grandfather and their father, and Pepin
shared it with his brother in the greatest harmony. Carloman then
relinquished the heavy burden of administering a temporal kingdom
and went off to Rome in search of peace, exactly for what reasons it
is not known, but apparently because he was fired by a love of the
contemplative life. He changed his dress, became a monk, built a
monastery on Monte Soracte beside the church of Saint Sylvester,
and there, in the company of the brethren who had come to join him
for the same reason, enjoyed for some years the peace for which he
longed. However, many noblemen from the land of the Franks kept
journeying to Rome in the performance of their vows, as the custom
is, and they were loath to miss visiting the man who had once been
their lord. By their never-ending payment of respects they interrupted
the calm which Carloman enjoyed so much and forced him to
change his dwelling place. As soon as he realized that the perpetual
repetition of this sort of thing must inevitably interfere with his plan,
he left his mountain retreat and went off to the province of Samnium
and the monastery of Saint Benedict on Monte Cassino, and there he
passed in the religious life what remained of his earthly existence.*

* Carloman died in 755.

By the authority of the Pope of Rome, from being Mayor of the Palace, Pepin was made King. He ruled alone over the Franks for fifteen years or more. Once he had finished the war in Aquitaine, which he had undertaken against Waifar, Duke of that country, and waged for nine consecutive years, Pepin died of dropsy in Paris [24 September 768]. Two sons survived him, Charlemagne and Carloman, and on these the succession of the kingship devolved by divine right. A general assembly was convened, according to custom, and the Franks appointed the two of them to be their Kings, on the express condition that they should divide the whole kingdom equally, Charlemagne taking over the government of the part which their father Pepin had held and Carloman the part which their uncle Carloman had ruled.

These conditions were accepted on both sides and each received the half of the kingdom which had been allotted to him in this way. This harmony continued between them, but with great difficulty, for many of the partisans of Carloman did their best to break up the alliance, to the point that certain of them even plotted to engage the two in warfare. However, the course of events proved that this danger was more imaginary than real, for Carloman died, and his wife and sons, together with a number of men who had been the leaders among his nobles, fled to Italy. There, for no particular reason, except perhaps scorn for her husband's brother, the widow placed herself and her children with her, under the protection of Desiderius, King of the Longobards.

After having ruled the kingdom conjointly with Charlemagne for two years, Carloman died [December 771] of some disease.* Once his brother was dead, Charlemagne was elected King with the consent of all the Franks.

* He had reigned for three years.

BOOK II

THE WARS AND POLITICAL
AFFAIRS OF CHARLEMAGNE

I consider that it would be foolish for me to write about Charlemagne's birth and childhood, or even about his boyhood, for nothing is set down in writing about this and nobody can be found still alive who claims to have any personal knowledge of these matters. I have therefore decided to leave out what is not really known and to move on to his deeds and habits and the other aspects of his life which need explanation and elaboration. First of all I shall describe his achievements at home and abroad, then his personal habits and enthusiasms, then the way in which he administered his kingdom, and last of all his death, omitting from all this nothing which ought to be known or, indeed, which is worthy of being recorded.

Of all the wars which Charlemagne waged, the first which he ever undertook was one against Aquitaine, which had been begun by his father but not brought to a proper conclusion. He thought that it would soon be over. He began it while his brother Carloman was still alive and even went so far as to ask his brother for help. Carloman did not give him the promised support; nevertheless Charlemagne pressed on energetically with the expedition which he had put into the field, refusing to withdraw from a campaign already started or to abandon a task once undertaken. In the end, with no small perseverance and continued effort, he brought to complete fruition what he was striving to achieve. After the death of Waifar [768], Hunold* had attempted to occupy Aquitaine and to renew a war which was almost over, but Charlemagne forced him to evacuate the territory and flee to Gascony. Determined as he was not to let Hunold find refuge there, Charlemagne crossed the River Garonne and sent messengers to Lupus, Duke of the Gascons, to

* Not Duke Hunold, father of Waifar, who had spent many years as a monk on the Ile de Rhé.

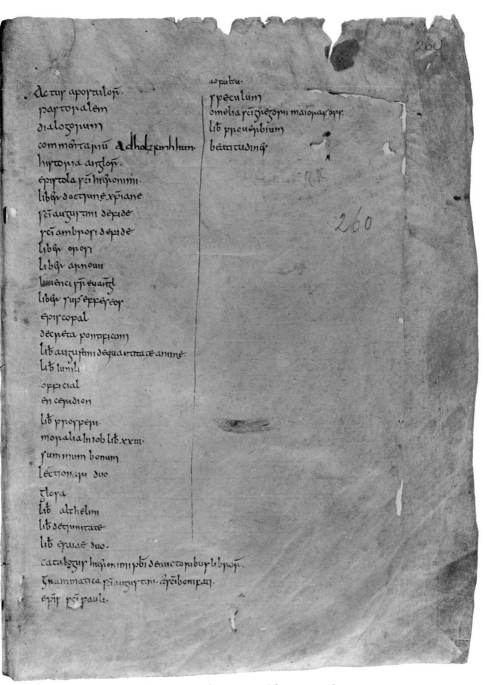

A page from a ninth-century library catalogue

order him to surrender the fugitive. Charlemagne threatened to declare war on Lupus, too, if he did not do as he was ordered quickly. Lupus made a sensible decision: not only did he surrender Hunold, but he also submitted himself and the province over which he ruled to Charlemagne's suzerainty.

Once matters were settled in Aquitaine and this particular war was finished, and now that his partner on the throne had been withdrawn from the anxieties of this world, Charlemagne next fought a war against the Longobards. He undertook this at the request of Hadrian, Bishop of the City of Rome, who first asked and then begged him to do so. This war, too, had been started in the first instance by Charlemagne's father, at the request of Pope Stephen, but in the most difficult circumstances, for certain of the Frankish leaders, whom Pepin the Short was accustomed to consult, were so opposed to his wishes that they openly announced their determination to desert their King and return home. Despite this Pepin declared war on King Haistulf and brought this war to a rapid completion. Although the reason for his undertaking the war was similar to that which had inspired his father, and indeed identical, it is clear that Charlemagne fought it with much more energy and brought it to a different conclusion. After besieging Pavia for a few days,* Pepin forced Haistulf to give hostages, to restore the towns and fortresses which he had taken from the Romans, and to swear an oath on the holy sacrament that he would not try to regain what he had surrendered. Once Charlemagne, on the other hand, had taken over the war, he did not stop until he had worn Desiderius down by a long siege and had received his surrender. He forced Adalgis, the son of Desiderius, on whom the hopes of everyone seemed to centre, to go into exile, not merely from his father's kingdom but indeed from Italy itself; he restored to the Romans everything which had been taken from them; he crushed a revolt started by Rotgaud, the Duke of Friuli,† subjected the whole of Italy to his own domination and made his son Pepin King of the territory which he had conquered. At this point I really should explain how difficult Charlemagne found the crossing of the Alps when he came to enter Italy, and after what effort on the part of the Franks the

---

* A gross understatement. In effect Pepin invaded Italy twice, in 754 and 756.

† The brief war with Rotgaud, Duke of Friuli, occurred some two years after the fall of Pavia.

pathless ridges of the mountains were traversed, and the rocks which reared themselves up to the sky and the abrupt abysses; but in this present work I am determined to offer the modern reader a description of Charlemagne's way of life and not the day-to-day details of his wars. The outcome of this conflict was that Italy was subdued, King Desiderius was carried off into exile for the remainder of his life, his son Adalgis was expelled from Italy and everything stolen by the Longobard Kings was restored to Hadrian, the ruler of the Church of Rome.*

Now that the war in Italy was over, the one against the Saxons, which had been interrupted for the time being, was taken up once more.† No war ever undertaken by the Frankish people was more prolonged, more full of atrocities or more demanding of effort. The Saxons, like almost all the peoples living in Germany, are ferocious by nature. They are much given to devil worship and they are hostile to our religion. They think it no dishonour to violate and transgress the laws of God and man. Hardly a day passed without some incident or other which was well calculated to break the peace. Our borders and theirs were contiguous and nearly everywhere in flat, open country, except, indeed, for a few places where great forests or mountain ranges interposed to separate the territories of the two peoples by a clear demarcation line. Murder, robbery and arson were of constant occurrence on both sides. In the end, the Franks were so irritated by these incidents that they decided that the time had come to abandon retaliatory measures and to undertake a full-scale war against these Saxons.

War was duly declared against them. It was waged for thirty-three long years and with immense hatred on both sides, but the losses of the Saxons were greater than those of the Franks. This war could have been brought to a more rapid conclusion, had it not been for the faithlessness of the Saxons. It is hard to say just how many times they were beaten and surrendered as suppliants to Charlemagne, promising to do all that was exacted from them, giving the hostages who were demanded, and this without delay, and receiving the ambassadors who were sent to them. Sometimes they were so cowed and reduced that they even promised to abandon their devil worship and submit willingly to the Christian faith; but, however ready they

* Desiderius remained until his death in the monastery of Corbie.
† The Saxon wars lasted from 772 until 804.

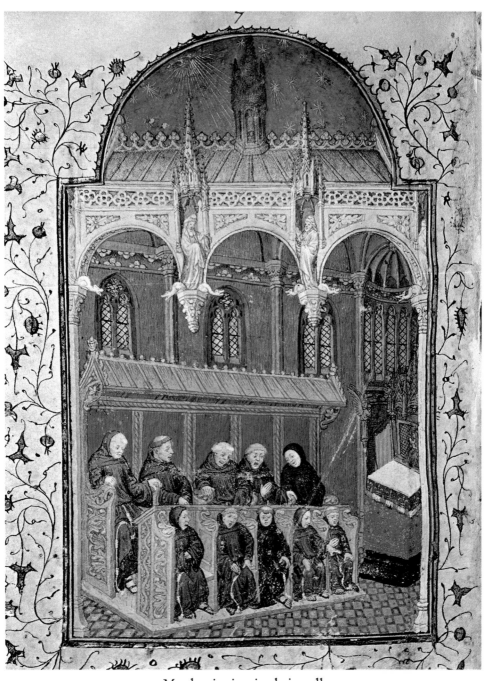

Monks singing in their stalls

might seem from time to time to do all this, they were always prepared to break the promises they had made. I cannot really judge which of these two courses can be said to have come the more easily to the Saxons, for, since the very beginning of the war against them, hardly a year passed in which they did not vacillate between surrender and defiance.

However, the King's mettlesome spirit and his imperturbability, which remained as constant in adversity as in prosperity, were not to be quelled by their ever-changing tactics, or, indeed, to be wearied by a task which he had once undertaken. Not once did he allow anyone who had offended in this way to go unpunished. He took vengeance on them for their perfidy and meted out suitable punish-ment, either by means of an army which he led himself or by dispatching a force against them under the command of his counts. In the end, when all those who had been offering resistance had been utterly defeated and subjected to his power, he transported some ten thousand men, taken from among those who lived both on this side of the Elbe and across the river, and dispersed them in small groups, with their wives and children, in various parts of Gaul and Germany. At long last this war, which had dragged on for so many years, came to an end on conditions imposed by the King and accepted by the Saxons. These last were to give up their devil worship and the malpractices inherited from their forefathers; and then, once they had adopted the sacraments of the Christian faith and religion, they were to be united with the Franks and become one people with them.

Despite the fact that it dragged on for so long, Charlemagne him-self did not meet the enemy in fixed battle more than twice in the course of this war,* once near Mount Osning in a placed called Detmold [783] and a second time [near Osnabrück] on the River Haase [783]. These two battles were fought in the course of one month, with only a few days' interval between them. In them the enemy were so beaten and cowed that they never again dared to attack the King, or even to resist his advance, except when they were safe behind the earthwork of some fortified place. In this conflict there were destroyed many Frankish and Saxon nobles who held the highest positions in the state. Finally it came to an end only in its thirty-third year, although in the interim many other great wars had started up against the Franks in various parts of the world. These

* Charlemagne also met the Saxons in battle near Lübeck in 775 and at Bochult in 779.

were directed by Charlemagne with such skill that anyone who studies them may well wonder which he ought to admire most, the King's endurance in time of travail, or his good fortune. This particular war against the Saxons began two years before the Italian campaign; and although Charlemagne pressed on with it unremittingly, no intermission was permitted in the wars being fought elsewhere, nor was a truce contemplated in any other military operation of comparable importance. Charlemagne was by far the most able and noble-spirited of all those who ruled over the nations in his time. He never withdrew from an enterprise which he had once begun and was determined to see through to the end, simply because of the labour involved; and danger never deterred him. Having learnt to endure and suffer each particular ineluctable circumstance, whatever its nature might be, he was never prepared to yield to adversity; and in times of prosperity he was never to be swayed by the false blandishments of fortune.

At a time when this war against the Saxons was being waged constantly and with hardly an intermission at all, Charlemagne left garrisons at strategic points along the frontier and went off himself with the largest force he could muster to invade Spain. He marched over a pass across the Pyrenees, received the surrender of every single town and castle which he attacked and then came back with his army safe and sound, except for the fact that for a brief moment on the return journey, while he was in the Pyrenean mountain range itself, he was given a taste of Basque treachery. Dense forests, which stretch in all directions, make this a spot most suitable for setting ambushes. At a moment when Charlemagne's army was stretched out in a long column of march, as the nature of the local defiles forced it to be, these Basques, who had set their ambush on the very top of one of the mountains, came rushing down on the last part of the baggage train and the troops who were marching in support of the rearguard and so protecting the army which had gone on ahead.* The Basques forced them down into the valley beneath, joined battle with them and killed them to the last man. They then snatched up the baggage, and, protected as they were by the cover of darkness, which was just beginning to fall, scattered in all directions without losing a moment. In this feat the Basques were helped by the lightness

* This is the battle of Roncevaux (so called since *La Chanson de Roland*) which took place on 15 August 778.

Charlemagne and his troops set off for Spain. The veterans from
Spain return to Aachen

of their arms and by the nature of the terrain in which the battle was fought. On the other hand, the heavy nature of their own equipment and the unevenness of the ground completely hampered the Franks in their resistance to the Basques. In this battle died Eggihard, who was in charge of the King's table, Anshelm, the Count of the Palace, and Roland, Lord of the Breton Marches, along with a great number of others. What is more, this assault could not be avenged there and then, for, once it was over, the enemy dispersed in such a way that no one knew where or among which people they could be found.

Charlemagne also subdued the Bretons,* who lived along the Ocean shore towards the West, in one of the extremities of Gaul. They refused to obey his command, so he sent an expedition against them. As a result they were forced to give hostages and promise to do whatever he ordered them. Next he set out himself for Italy with an army, marched through Rome and advanced as far as Capua, a town in Campania. He pitched his camp there and threatened to declare war on the men of Benevento unless they capitulated [786]. Areghis, their Duke, prevented this, for he sent his two sons Rumold and Grimold to meet the King, with a large sum of money. He begged the King to accept his sons as hostages and promised that he and his people would obey Charlemagne's orders, with this one reservation that he should not be compelled to come in person. Charlemagne decided that it was more important to consider the interests of the people than to worry about their Duke's obstinacy. He received the hostages and as a great favour agreed that the Duke should not be forced to appear before him. He kept one of the two sons of Areghis, the younger, and dispatched the older one back to his father. He sent messengers to demand and receive oaths of fidelity from the Beneventans and from Areghis himself. Then he made his way back to Rome, spent some few days there in his personal devotions at the holy places, and so returned to Gaul.

Next there suddenly broke out a war in Bavaria [787], but this was very soon over. It was occasioned by the pride and folly of Duke Tassilo. He was encouraged by his wife, who was the daughter of King Desiderius and thought that through her husband she could revenge her father's exile, to make an alliance with the

* This victory in 786, by Audulf, was short-lived. Wido beat the Bretons in 799, and they offered their allegiance to Charlemagne at Tours in 800; but they were once more in revolt in 811.

Huns [Avars], the neighbours of the Bavarians to the East. Not only did Tassilo refuse to carry out Charlemagne's orders, but he did his utmost to provoke the King to war. Tassilo's arrogance was too much for the spirited King of the Franks to stomach. Charlemagne summoned his levies from all sides and himself marched against Bavaria with a huge army, coming to the River Lech, which divides the Bavarians from the Germans. He pitched his camp on the bank of this river. Before he invaded the province he determined to dis-cover the intentions of the Duke by sending messengers to him. Tassilo realized that nothing could be gained for himself or his people by his remaining stubborn. He went in person to beg Charlemagne's forgiveness, handed over the hostages who had been demanded, his own son Theodo among them, and, what is more, swore an oath that he would never again listen to anyone who might try to persuade him to revolt against the King's authority. In this way a war which had all the appearance of becoming very serious was in the event brought to a swift conclusion. Tassilo was summoned to the King's presence and was not allowed to go back home after-wards.* The government of the province over which he had ruled was entrusted from that moment onwards not to a single duke but to a group of counts.

No sooner were these troubles over than Charlemagne declared war on the Slavs, whom we are accustomed to call Wiltzes, but whose real name, in their own language, is the Welatabi. In this conflict the Saxons fought as allies alongside certain other nations who followed Charlemagne's standards, although their loyalty was feigned and far from sincere. The cause of the war was that the Welatabi refused to obey Charlemagne's orders and kept harassing with never-ending invasions the Abodrites, who earlier on had been allied to the Franks.

From the Western Ocean there stretches eastwards an arm of the sea of unknown length, nowhere exceeding a hundred miles in width, and, indeed, much narrower in many places.† Round this sea live many peoples. The Danes and the Swedes, whom we call the Northmen, occupy its northern shore and all its islands. The Slavs, the Esthonians and various other nations inhabit its eastern shore; and outstanding among these are the Welatabi, against whom

---

* Duke Tassilo was forced to become a monk in the monastery of Jumièges.

† The Baltic is some 850–900 miles in length and 100–200 miles wide.

Charlemagne in his tent at the siege of Pamplona

the King was now waging war. A single campaign [789], which Charlemagne directed himself, sufficed to crush and tame them, so that they never again dreamed of disobeying his orders.*

The war which came next was the most important which Charlemagne ever fought, except the one against the Saxons: I mean the struggle with the Avars or Huns. He waged it with more vigour than any of the others and with much greater preparation. He himself led only one expedition into Pannonia the province which the Huns occupied at that period. Everything else he entrusted to his son Pepin, to the governors of his provinces and to his counts and legates. The war was prosecuted with great vigour by these men and it came to an end in its eighth year.†

Just how many battles were fought and how much blood was shed is shown by the fact that Pannonia is now completely uninhabited and that the site of the Khan's palace is now so deserted that no evidence remains that anyone ever lived there. All the Hun nobility died in this war, all their glory departed. All their wealth and their treasures assembled over so many years were dispersed. The memory of man cannot recall any war against the Franks by which they were so enriched and their material possessions so increased. These Franks, who until then had seemed almost paupers, now discovered so much gold and silver in the palace and captured so much precious booty in their battles, that it could rightly be maintained that they had in all justice taken from the Huns what these last had unjustly stolen from other nations.

Only two of the Frankish nobles died in this war: Eric, Duke of Friuli,‡ who was surprised by an ambush of townsfolk in Liburnia, near the maritime city of Tersatto; and Gerold, the Governor of Bavaria, who was slain in Pannonia by an unknown hand, together with two men who formed his sole escort when, just before a conflict with the Huns, he was drawing up his line of battle and riding ahead to encourage each of his troops by name. Otherwise this war was almost bloodless as far as the Franks were concerned and its outcome was most fortunate, although, because of its importance, it lasted so long.

* The Wiltzes rose in rebellion again in 808.

† In effect the war against the Avars lasted from 791 until 803.

‡ The death of Eric, Duke of Friuli, in 799, was not connected with the war against the Avars.

Subsequently the Saxon war, too, ended in a settlement which matched its drawn-out nature. Wars in Bohemia [805] and Luneburg came next, but they did not last long; they were both brought to a swift conclusion under the direction of the young Charles.*

The last war which Charlemagne undertook was against those Northmen who are called Danes [804-10]. They first came as pirates and then they ravaged the coasts of Gaul and Germany with a large fleet. Their King Godefrid was so puffed up with empty ambition that he planned to make himself master of the whole of Germany. He had come to look upon Frisia and Saxony as provinces belonging to him; and he had already reduced the Abodrites, who were his neighbours, to a state of subservience and made them pay him tribute. Now he boasted that he would soon come with a huge army to Aachen itself, where the King had his court. There was no lack of people to believe his boasting, however empty it really was. He was really considered to be on the point of trying some such manœuvre, and was only prevented from doing so by the fact that he died suddenly. He was killed by one of his own followers, so that his own life and the war which he had started both came to a sudden end.

These, then, are the wars which this powerful King Charlemagne waged with such prudence and success in various parts of the world throughout a period of forty-seven years, that is during the whole of his reign. The Frankish kingdom which he inherited from his father Pepin was already far-flung and powerful. By these wars of his he increased it to such an extent that he added to it almost as much again. Originally no more land was occupied by the Eastern Franks, as they were called, than the region of Gaul which lies between the Rhine, the Loire, the Atlantic Ocean and the sea round the Balearic Islands, together with the part of Germany which is situated between Saxony, the Danube, the Rhine and the Saal, which last river divides the Thuringians and the Sorabians. To this must be added, too, the fact that the Alamanni and the Bavarians formed part of the Frankish kingdom. By the campaigns which I have described, Charlemagne annexed Aquitaine,† Gascony, the whole mountain range of the Pyrenees and land stretching as far south as the River

* The war against the Linonici, in 808, was not successful, and they rose again in 811.

† Einhard adds Aquitaine to make Charlemagne's achievements more impressive.

The battle of Roncevaux, as a fifteenth-century miniaturist imagined it

Ebro, which rises in Navarre, flows through the most fertile plains of Spain and then enters the Balearic Sea beneath the walls of the city of Tortosa.* He added the whole of Italy, which stretches for a thousand miles and more in length from Aosta to southern Calabria,† at the point where the frontiers between the Greeks and the men of Benevento are to be found. To this he joined Saxony, which forms a very considerable part of Germany and is considered to be twice as wide as the territory occupied by the Franks, while it is just about as long; then both provinces of Pannonia, the part of Dacia which is beyond the Danube, Istria, Liburnia and Dalmatia, with the exception of its maritime cities, which Charlemagne allowed the Emperor of Constantinople to keep, in view of his friendship with him and the treaty which he had made. Finally he tamed and forced to pay tribute all the wild and barbarous nations which inhabit Germany between the Rivers Rhine and Vistula, the Atlantic Ocean and the Danube, peoples who are almost identical in their language, although they differ greatly in habit and customs. Among these last the most notable are the Welatabi, the Sorabians, the Abodrites and the Bohemians, against all of whom he waged war; the others, by far the greater number, surrendered without a struggle.

In addition to all this, Charlemagne made his reign more glorious by the friendly relations which he established with certain kings and peoples who became favourably inclined towards him. For example, Alfonso II, the King of Galicia and Asturias, became so close a friend that, when he had occasion to send letters or messengers to Charlemagne,‡ he ordered that he should always be called the King's own man. By the rich gifts which he gave them, Charlemagne had so influenced the Kings of the Irish that they never addressed him as anything else but their lord, and called themselves his slaves and subjects. There exist letters which they sent to him in which this subservience towards him is clearly shown.§

With Harun-al-Rachid, King of the Persians, who held almost

* Charlemagne did not take Tortosa, and his Empire did not extend to the Ebro.
† A further exaggeration.
‡ No such letters exist.
§ Again no such letters exist. In any case, Einhard may mean Eardulf, King of Northumbria, rather than the kings of the Irish. On the other hand, Charlemagne certainly had diplomatic relations with the Irish.

the whole of the East in fee, always excepting India, Charlemagne was on such friendly terms that Harun valued his goodwill more than the approval of all the other kings and princes in the entire world, and considered that he alone was worthy of being honoured and propitiated with gifts.* When Charlemagne's messengers, whom he had sent with offerings to the most Holy Sepulchre of our Lord and Saviour and to the place of His resurrection, came to Harun and told him of their master's intention, he not only granted all that was asked but even went so far as to agree that this sacred scene of our redemption should be placed under Charlemagne's own jurisdiction. When the time came for these messengers to turn home-wards, Harun sent some of his own men to accompany them and dispatched to Charlemagne costly gifts, which included robes, spices and other marvels of the lands of the Orient. A few years earlier Harun had sent Charlemagne the only elephant he possessed, simply because the Frankish King asked for it.

In the same way the Emperors of Constantinople, Nicephorus I, Michael I and Leo V, sought Charlemagne's friendship and alliance of their own free will, and sent many messengers to him.† When he accepted the title of Emperor, he aroused their strong suspicion, for he might well have been planning to take their own imperial power from them; but he concluded a firm treaty with them, in order to prevent any possible cause of dissension from arising between them. All the same, the power of the Franks always seemed suspect to the Greeks and Romans. Hence the Greek proverb which is still quoted today: If a Frank is your friend, then he is clearly not your neighbour.

However much energy Charlemagne may have expended in

---

* Charlemagne sent an ambassador to the Holy Sepulchre in 799. When this ambassador returned in November 800, he brought from the Patriarch of Jerusalem, not from Harun-al-Rachid (Caliph of Bagdad, 786–809), the Keys of the Holy Sepulchre and of Mount Calvary, as a sign of deference, not as a surrender of juris-diction. In 801 ambassadors to Charlemagne from Harun-al-Rachid landed at Pisa, and not long after arrived the elephant, Abu-l-Abbas, which lived until 810. Einhard seems to have invented the story that this was the only elephant in Harun's possession! It was not until 807 that a new embassy arrived from Harun-al-Rachid, with rich materials, spices, and, although Einhard does not mention them, a water-clock, candelabra and a tent. As he does so often, Einhard is misreading his prime source and telescoping the details.

† Nicephorus I was Emperor 802–811, Michael I 811–13 and Leo V 813–20. The messengers from Leo V did not arrive until after Charlemagne's death.

Trou uolnt saunne ce ce carlos ymaie.
Dist qil leueule sauon par gise ce mesaie.
Son escriueis enuoie ce mot par estoit saie.
Vn breus liseit escriue elle romas legnie.
E pst .ij. chos ce mels ce son bnage.

Aportes moi cist breus afanchois auane.
E qui uos responnita remenes encoraie.
Celes partiret alaule sa coilet lor uoiage.
E tut oit esploits por plans 7 por loschaie.
Q eil ueret paus los cors 7 li estuie.
Par ce fois la ate3 ueret couerr les baie.
Oe sece 7 ce cules ce cœr dinis depaine.
Cil lor auoit Rollat acoplis son uiaie.
Oe Rome estoit tornes si amena el bnage.
E ce part la postoile salue lemprime.
Suat ce arles ce made Rollat li gns capaine.
Con le feit la postoille il asa get Romaine.

Foreign envoys bring a message to Charlemagne

enlarging his realm and conquering foreign nations, and despite all the time which he devoted to this preoccupation, he nevertheless set in hand many projects which aimed at making his kingdom more attractive and at increasing public utility. Some of these projects he completed. Outstanding among these, one might claim, are the great church of the Holy Mother of God at Aachen, which is a really remarkable construction, and the bridge over the Rhine at Mainz, which is five hundred feet long, this being the width of the river at that point. The bridge was burned down just one year before Charlemagne's death. He planned to rebuild it in stone instead of wood, but his death followed so quickly that the bridge could not be restored in time. He also began the construction of two magnificent palaces: one not far from the city of Mainz, near the township called Ingelheim; and the other at Nimeguen, on the River Waal, which flows along the southern shore of the Betuwa peninsula. More important still was the fact that he commanded the bishops and churchmen in whose care they were to restore sacred edifices which had fallen into ruin through their very antiquity, wherever he discovered them throughout the whole of his kingdom; and he instructed his representatives to see that these orders were carried out.

Charlemagne took upon himself the task of building a fleet to ward off the attacks of the Northmen. For this purpose ships were constructed near to the rivers which flow out of Gaul and Germany into the North Sea. In view of the fact that these Northmen kept on attacking and pillaging the coast of Gaul and Germany, Charlemagne placed strong-points and coastguard stations at all the ports and at the mouths of all rivers considered large enough for the entry of ships, so that the enemy could be bottled up by this military task force. He did the same in the south, along the shore of southern Gaul and Septimania, and along the whole coast of Italy as far north as Rome, against the Moors who had recently begun piratical attacks. The result of this measure was that during his lifetime no serious damage was done to Italy by the Moors, or to Gaul and Germany by the Northmen. The only exceptions were Civitavecchia, a city in Etruria, which was captured and sacked by the Moors as the result of treachery; and certain islands in Frisia, near to the German coast, which were looted by the Northmen.

BOOK III

THE EMPEROR'S PRIVATE LIFE

What has gone before is a fair picture of Charlemagne and all that he did to protect and enlarge his kingdom, and indeed to embellish it. I shall now speak of his intellectual qualities, his extraordinary strength of character, whether in prosperity or adversity, and all the other details of his personal and domestic life.

After the death of his father, at the time when he was sharing the kingship with Carloman, Charlemagne bore with such patience this latter's hatred and jealousy that everyone was surprised that he never lost his temper with his brother.

Then, at the bidding of his mother, he married the daughter of Desiderius, the King of the Longobards.* Nobody knows why, but he dismissed this wife after one year. Next he married Hildigard, a woman of most noble family, from the Swabian race. By her he had three sons, Charles, Pepin and Lewis, and the same number of daughters, Rotrude, Bertha and Gisela.† He had three more daughters, Theoderada, Hiltrude and Rothaide, two of these by his third wife, Fastrada, who was from the race of Eastern Franks or Germans,‡ and the last by a concubine whose name I cannot remember. Fastrada died and he married Liutgard, from the Alamanni, but she bore him no children.§ After Liutgard's death, he took four concubines: Madelgard, who bore him a daughter Ruothilde; Gersvinda, of the Saxon race, by whom he had a daughter Adaltrude; Regina, who bore him Drogo¶

* This first marriage probably took place in 770.

† Hildigard died on 30 April 783. By her Charlemagne had four sons and four daughters, according to Paul the Deacon: one son, the twin of Lewis, called Lothar, died as a baby and is not mentioned by Einhard; two daughters, Hildigard and Adelhaid, died as babies, so that Einhard seems to err in one of his names, unless there were really five daughters.

‡ Fastrada, Charlemagne's third wife, died in 794.

§ Liutgard, the fourth wife, died in 800.

¶ Drogo was Archbishop of Metz from 823 to 855.

Lewis the Pious, son of Charlemagne

and Hugo;* and Adallinda, who became the mother of Theodoric.

Charlemagne's own mother, Bertrada, lived with him in high honour to a very great age. He treated her with every respect and never had a cross word with her, except over the divorce of King Desiderius' daughter, whom he had married on her advice. Bertrada died soon after Hildigard [12 July 783], living long enough to see three grandsons and as many granddaughters in her son's house. Charlemagne buried her with great honour in the church of Saint Denis, where his father lay.

He had a single sister, Gisela by name, who from her childhood onwards had been dedicated to the religious life.† He treated her with the same respect which he showed his mother. She died a few years before Charlemagne himself, in the nunnery where she had spent her life.

Charlemagne was determined to give his children, his daughters just as much as his sons, a proper training in the liberal arts which had formed the subject of his own studies. As soon as they were old enough he had his sons taught to ride in the Frankish fashion, to use arms and to hunt. He made his daughters learn to spin and weave wool, use the distaff and spindle, and acquire every womanly accomplishment, rather than fritter away their time in sheer idleness.

Of all his children he lost only two sons and one daughter prior to his own death.‡ These were his eldest son Charles [4 December 811], Pepin whom he had made King of Italy,§ and Rotrude [6 June 810], the eldest of his daughters, who had been engaged to Constantine, the Emperor of the Greeks. Pepin left one son, called Bernard, and five daughters, Adelhaid, Atula, Gundrada, Berthaid and Theoderada. Charlemagne gave clear proof of the affection which he bore them all, for after the death of Pepin he ordered his grandson Bernard to succeed and he had his granddaughters brought up with his own girls. He bore the death of his two sons and his daughter with less fortitude than one would have expected, considering the strength of his character; for his emotions as a father, which were very deeply rooted, made him burst into tears.

When the death of Hadrian [796], the Pope of Rome and his close

---

* Hugo became Abbot of the monastery of Saint Quentin and died in 844.

† Gisela was Abbess of the convent of Chelles, Seine-et-Marne.

‡ This omits the children who died young.

§ Pepin had been King of Italy since 781. He died on 8 July 810.

friend, was announced to him, he wept as if he had lost a brother or a dearly loved son. He was firm and steady in his human relation-ships, developing friendship easily, keeping it up with care and doing everything he possibly could for anyone whom he had admitted to this degree of intimacy.

He paid such attention to the upbringing of his sons and daughters that he never sat down to table without them when he was at home, and never set out on a journey without taking them with him. His sons rode at his side and his daughters followed along behind. Hand-picked guards watched over them as they closed the line of march. These girls were extraordinarily beautiful and greatly loved by their father. It is a remarkable fact that, as a result of this, he kept them with him in his household until the very day of his death, instead of giving them in marriage to his own men or to foreigners, maintaining that he could not live without them. The consequence was that he had a number of unfortunate experiences,* he who had been so lucky in all else that he undertook. However, he shut his eyes to all that happened, as if no suspicion of any immoral conduct had ever reached him, or as if the rumour was without foundation.

I did not mention with the others a son called Pepin who was born to Charlemagne by a concubine [Himiltrude]. He was hand-some enough, but a hunchback. At a moment when his father was wintering in Bavaria, soon after the beginning of his campaign [792] against the Huns, this Pepin pretended to be ill and conspired with certain of the Frankish leaders who had won him over to their cause by pretending to offer him the kingship. The plot was discovered and the conspirators were duly punished. Pepin was tonsured and permitted to take up, in the monastery of Prüm, the life of a religious for which he had already expressed a vocation.

Earlier on there had been another dangerous conspiracy against Charlemagne in Germany.† All the plotters were exiled, some having their eyes put out first, but the others were not maltreated physically. Only three of them were killed. These resisted arrest, drew their swords and started to defend themselves. They slaughtered

---

* By Count Rorigo Rotrude had an illegitimate son called Lewis, who became Abbot of Saint Denis. Bertha had several illegitimate children, among them the historian Nithard, by the poet Angilbert, whom Charlemagne addressed as Homer and who later became Abbot of Saint Riquier.

† The revolt of Hardrad in 785–6.

Charlemagne with his sister Gisela and Saint Giles

a few men in the process and had to be destroyed themselves, as there was no other way of dealing with them.

The cruelty of Queen Fastrada is thought to have been the cause of both these conspiracies, since it was under her influence that Charlemagne seemed to have taken actions which were fundamentally opposed to his normal kindliness and good nature.* Throughout the remainder of his life he so won the love and favour of all his fellow human beings, both at home and abroad, that no one ever levelled against him the slightest charge of cruelty or injustice.

He loved foreigners and took great pains to make them welcome. So many visited him as a result that they were rightly held to be a burden not only to the palace, but to the entire realm. In his magnanimity he took no notice at all of this criticism, for he considered that his reputation for hospitality and the advantage of the good name which he acquired more than compensated for the great nuisance of their being there.

The Emperor was strong and well built.† He was tall in stature, but not excessively so, for his height was just seven times the length of his own feet. The top of his head was round, and his eyes were piercing and unusually large. His nose was slightly longer than normal, he had a fine head of white hair and his expression was gay and good-humoured. As a result, whether he was seated or standing, he always appeared masterful and dignified. His neck was short and rather thick, and his stomach a trifle too heavy, but the proportions of the rest of his body prevented one from noticing these blemishes. His step was firm and he was manly in all his movements. He spoke distinctly, but his voice was thin for a man of his physique. His health was good, except that he suffered from frequent attacks of fever during the last four years of his life, and towards the end he was lame in one foot. Even then he continued to do exactly as he wished, instead of following the advice of his doctors, whom he came positively to dislike after they advised him to stop eating the roast meat to which he was accustomed and to live on stewed dishes.

He spent much of his time on horseback and out hunting, which

* The main act of cruelty remembered against Charlemagne was the hanging of 4,500 Saxon rebels in one day at Verden in 782, and this was before his marriage with Fastrada.

† Many of these details are taken from what Suetonius had said about Caesar, Augustus, Tiberius, Claudius and Nero!

came naturally to him, for it would be difficult to find another race on earth who could equal the Franks in this activity. He took delight in steam-baths at the thermal springs, and loved to exercise himself in the water whenever he could. He was an extremely strong swimmer and in this sport no one could surpass him. It was for this reason that he built his palace at Aachen and remained continuously in residence there during the last years of his life and indeed until the moment of his death. He would invite not only his sons to bathe with him, but his nobles and friends as well, and occasionally even a crowd of his attendants and bodyguards, so that sometimes a hundred men or more would be in the water together.

He wore the national dress of the Franks. Next to his skin he had a linen shirt and linen drawers; and then long hose and a tunic edged with silk. He wore shoes on his feet and bands of cloth wound round his legs. In winter he protected his chest and shoulders with a jerkin made of otter skins or ermine. He wrapped himself in a blue cloak and always had a sword strapped to his side, with a hilt and belt of gold or silver. Sometimes he would use a jewelled sword, but this was only on great feast days or when ambassadors came from foreign peoples. He hated the clothes of other countries, no matter how becoming they might be, and he would never consent to wear them. The only exception to this was one day in Rome when Pope Hadrian entreated him to put on a long tunic and a Greek mantle, and to wear shoes made in the Roman fashion; and then a second time, when Leo, Hadrian's successor, persuaded him to do the same thing. On feast days he walked in procession in a suit of cloth of gold, with jewelled shoes, his cloak fastened with a golden brooch and with a crown of gold and precious stones on his head. On ordinary days his dress differed hardly at all from that of the common people.

He was moderate in his eating and drinking, and especially so in drinking; for he hated to see drunkenness in any man, and even more so in himself and his friends. All the same, he could not go long without food, and he often used to complain that fasting made him feel ill. He rarely gave banquets and these only on high feast days, but then he would invite a great number of guests. His main meal of the day was served in four courses, in addition to the roast meat which his hunters used to bring in on spits and which he enjoyed more than any other food. During his meal he would listen

A sword which is supposed to have belonged to Charlemagne

to a public reading or some other entertainment. Stories would be recited for him, or the doings of the ancients told again. He took great pleasure in the books of Saint Augustine and especially in those which are called *The City of God*.

He was so sparing in his use of wine and every other beverage that he rarely drank more than three times in the course of his dinner. In summer, after his midday meal, he would eat some fruit and take another drink; then he would remove his shoes and undress completely, just as he did at night, and rest for two or three hours. During the night he slept so lightly that he would wake four or five times and rise from his bed. When he was dressing and putting on his shoes he would invite his friends to come in. Moreover, if the Count of the Palace told him that there was some dispute which could not be settled without the Emperor's personal decision, he would order the disputants to be brought in there and then, hear the case as if he were sitting in tribunal and pronounce a judgement. If there was any official business to be transacted on that day, or any order to be given to one of his ministers, he would settle it at the same time.

He spoke easily and fluently, and could express with great clarity whatever he had to say. He was not content with his own mother tongue, but took the trouble to learn foreign languages. He learnt Latin so well that he spoke it as fluently as his own tongue; but he understood Greek better than he could speak it. He was eloquent to the point of sometimes seeming almost garrulous.

He paid the greatest attention to the liberal arts; and he had great respect for men who taught them, bestowing high honours upon them. When he was learning the rules of grammar he received tuition from Peter the Deacon of Pisa, who by then was an old man, but for all other subjects he was taught by Alcuin, surnamed Albinus, another Deacon, a man of the Saxon race who came from Britain and was the most learned man anywhere to be found. Under him the Emperor spent much time and effort in studying rhetoric, dialectic and especially astrology. He applied himself to mathematics and traced the course of the stars with great attention and care. He also tried to learn to write. With this object in view he used to keep writing-tablets and notebooks under the pillows on his bed, so that he could try his hand at forming letters during his leisure moments; but, although he tried very hard, he had begun too late in life and he made little progress.

Charlemagne practised the Christian religion with great devotion and piety, for he had been brought up in this faith since earliest childhood. This explains why he built a cathedral of such great beauty at Aachen, decorating it with gold and silver, with lamps, and with lattices and doors of solid bronze.* He was unable to find marble columns for his construction anywhere else, and so he had them brought from Rome and Ravenna.†

As long as his health lasted he went to church morning and evening with great regularity, and also for early morning Mass, and the late-night hours.‡ He took the greatest pains to ensure that all church ceremonies were performed with the utmost dignity, and he was always warning the sacristans to see that nothing sordid or dirty was brought into the building or left there. He donated so many sacred vessels made of gold and silver, and so many priestly vestments, that when service time came even those who opened and closed the doors, surely the humblest of all church dignitaries, had no need to perform their duties in their everyday clothes.

He made careful reforms in the way in which the psalms were chanted and the lessons read. He was himself quite an expert at both of these exercises, but he never read the lesson in public and he would sing only with the rest of the congregation and then in a low voice.

He was most active in relieving the poor and in that form of really disinterested charity which the Greeks call *eleemosyna*. He gave alms not only in his own country and in the kingdom over which he reigned, but also across the sea in Syria, Egypt, Africa, Jerusalem, Alexandria and Carthage. Wherever he heard that Christians were living in want, he took pity on their poverty and sent them money regularly. It was, indeed, precisely for this reason that he sought the friendship of kings beyond the sea, for he hoped that some relief and alleviation might result for the Christians living under their domination.

Charlemagne cared more for the church of the holy Apostle Peter

* These doors are still to be seen in the great church at Aachen.

† There is still in existence a letter from Pope Hadrian I in which he authorizes Charlemagne to move marbles and mosaics from the palace in Ravenna to help him with his constructions in Aachen.

‡ There was only morning Mass. Charlemagne went, too, to morning, evening and late-night Hours.

Saint Augustine of Hippo, as imagined by a twelfth-century
miniaturist of Saint Augustine's Abbey, Canterbury

in Rome than for any other sacred and venerable place. He poured into its treasury a vast fortune in gold and silver coinage and in precious stones. He sent so many gifts to the Pope that it was impossible to keep count of them. Throughout the whole period of his reign nothing was ever nearer to his heart than that, by his own efforts and exertion, the city of Rome should regain its former proud position. His ambition was not merely that the church of Saint Peter should remain safe and protected thanks to him, but that by means of his wealth it should be more richly adorned and endowed than any other church. However much he thought of Rome, it still remains true that throughout his whole reign of forty-seven years he went there only four times to fulfil his vows and to offer up his prayers.

These were not the sole reasons for Charlemagne's last visit to Rome. The truth is that the inhabitants of Rome had violently attacked Pope Leo, putting out his eyes and cutting off his tongue, and had forced him to flee to the King for help.* Charlemagne really came to Rome to restore the Church, which was in a very bad state indeed, but in the end he spent the whole winter there. It was on this occasion that he received the title of Emperor and Augustus. At first he was far from wanting this. He made it clear that he would not have entered the cathedral that day at all, although it was the greatest of all the festivals of the Church, if he had known in advance what the Pope was planning to do. Once he had accepted the title, he endured with great patience the jealousy of the so-called Roman Emperors, who were most indignant at what had happened.† He overcame their hostility only by the sheer strength of his personality, which was much more powerful than theirs. He was for ever sending messengers to them, and in his dispatches he called them his brothers.

Now that he was Emperor, he discovered that there were many defects in the legal system of his own people, for the Franks have

---

* The attack on Leo III occurred on 25 April 799. An attempt was made to blind him and cut out his tongue; had it succeeded he would have been forced to give up all priestly offices. The Pope fled to Charlemagne's camp at Paderborn. Charlemagne came to Rome on 24 November 800. He was crowned Emperor in Saint Peter's on 25 December of that year.

† The Emperors of Constantinople considered themselves, with justification, to be the sole heirs of the Roman Emperors. In 800 the Empress Irene ruled in Constantinople.

two separate codes of law which differ from each other in many points.* He gave much thought to how he could best fill the gaps, reconcile the discrepancies, correct the errors and rewrite the laws, which were ill-expressed. None of this was ever finished; he added a few sections, but even these remained incomplete. What he did do was to have collected together and committed to writing the laws of all the nations under his jurisdiction which still remained unrecorded.

At the same time he directed that the age-old narrative poems, barbarous enough, it is true, in which were celebrated the warlike deeds of the kings of ancient times, should be written out and so preserved. He also began a grammar of his native tongue.†

He gave the months of the year suitable titles in his own tongue. Before his time the Franks had known some of these by Latin names and others by barbarian ones. He gave titles to the twelve winds, not more than four of which, if as many as that, had been distinguished before. To take the months first, he called January *wintarmanoth* [winter month], February *hornung* [turn of the year], March *lentzinmanoth* [renewal month or Lent], April *ostarmanoth* [Easter month], May *winnemanoth* [month of joy], June *brachmanoth* [month of ploughing], July *heuuimanoth* [hay month], August *aran-manoth* [month of the corn ears], September *witumanoth* [wood month], October *windumemanoth* [month of the wine harvest], November *herbistmanoth* [harvest month] and December *heilagmanoth* [Holy month]. He gave the following names to the winds: the east wind he called *ostroniwint*, the south-east wind *ostsundroni*, the south-south-east wind *sundostroni* and the south wind *sundroni*; he called the south-south-west wind *sundwestroni*, the south-west wind *westsundroni*, the west wind *westroni*, the north-west wind *westnordroni*, the north-north-west wind *nordwestroni*, the north wind *nordroni*, the north-north-east wind *nordostroni* and the north-east wind *ostnordroni*.

* The laws of the Salian Franks and those of the Ripuarian Franks.
† None of this remains.

The Molsheim brooch, made in the eighth century

BOOK IV

THE EMPEROR'S LAST YEARS
AND DEATH

At the very end of his life, when old age and illness were already weighing heavily upon him, Charlemagne summoned to his presence Lewis, the King of Aquitaine, the only surviving son of Hildigard. A council of the Frankish leaders was duly convened from the whole realm. With the agreement of all who attended, Charlemagne gave Lewis a half-share in his kingship and made him heir to the imperial title. He placed the crown on Lewis' head and ordered that he should be called Emperor and Augustus [11 September 813]. This decision of Charlemagne's was accepted with great enthusiasm by all who were there, for it seemed to have come to him as a divine inspiration for the welfare of the state. It increased Charlemagne's authority at home and at the same time it struck no small terror into the minds of foreign peoples.

Charlemagne then sent his son back to Aquitaine. He himself, although enfeebled by old age, went off hunting as usual,* but without moving far from his palace at Aachen. He passed what remained of the autumn in this way and then returned to Aachen towards the beginning of November. While he was spending the winter there, he was attacked by a sharp fever at some time in January and so took to his bed. As he always did when he had a temperature, he immediately cut down his diet, thinking that he could cure his fever by fasting, or at least alleviate it. He then developed a pain in the side, called pleurisy by the Greeks, in addition to the temperature. He continued his dieting, taking liquids as his only nourishment, and those at rare intervals. On the seventh day after he had taken to his bed he received Holy Communion, and then he died, at nine o'clock in the morning on 28 January, this being the

---

* Einhard, as so often, puts the events in the wrong sequence. Charlemagne went hunting in the Ardennes in the summer of 813, fell ill, and decided as a result to crown his son Lewis.

seventy-second year of his life and the forty-seventh year of his reign.*

His body was washed and prepared for burial in the usual way. It was then borne into the cathedral and interred there, amidst the great lamentation of the entire population. At first there had been some doubt as to where he should be buried, for he had given no directions about this during his lifetime. In the end it was agreed by all that no more suitable place could be found for his interment than the cathedral which he had built himself at his own expense in that town, for the love of God and of our Lord Jesus Christ, and in honour of His holy and ever-virgin Mother. He was buried there on the day of his death and a gilded arch with his statue and an inscrip-tion was raised above the tomb. The inscription ran as follows:

> Beneath this stone lies the body
> of Charles the Great, the Christian Emperor,
> who greatly expanded the kingdom of the Franks
> and reigned successfully for forty-seven years.
> He died when more than seventy years old
> in the eight hundred and fourteenth year
> of our Lord,
> in the seventh tax-year, on 28 January.

Many portents marked the approach of Charlemagne's death, so that not only other people but he himself could know that it was near.† In all three of the last years of his life there occurred repeatedly eclipses of both the sun and the moon; and a black-coloured spot was to be seen on the sun for seven days at a stretch. The immensely strong portico which he had constructed between his palace and the cathedral came crashing down to its very foundations one Ascension Day.‡ The wooden bridge across the Rhine near Mainz which he

---

* This implies that Charlemagne was born in 742. In the epitaph I have translated *septuagenarius* as 'more than seventy years old', to agree with this; but if Einhard really means 'seventy', then he is contradicting himself and making 744 the date of birth.

† Einhard had read of similar portents in the *Lives* of Augustus, Caligula and Claudius, as related by Suetonius. According to the *Annales regni Francorum*, there were in the year 806–807 three eclipses of the moon, one of the sun and a spot on the sun which lasted for eight days. There was an eclipse of the moon in 809, two eclipses of the moon and two of the sun in 810 and an eclipse of the sun in 812. Einhard tidies this up!

‡ The portico fell in 817, three years after Charlemagne's death.

A reliquary which is supposed to have belonged to the Saxon
Widukind in the late eighth century

had built over a period of ten years, with such immense skill and labour that it seemed likely to last for ever, caught fire by accident and was burnt out in three hours, to the point that not a single plank remained, except what was under the water.* What is more, one day during the last expedition which he led into Saxony against Godefrid [810], the King of the Danes, just before sunrise, as he was setting out from his camp and was beginning the day's march, he suddenly saw a meteor flash down from the heavens and pass across the clear sky from right to left with a great blaze of light. As everyone was staring at this portent and wondering what it meant, the horse which Charlemagne was riding suddenly lowered its head and fell, throwing him to the ground so violently that the buckle fastening his cloak was broken and his sword-belt torn away. He was picked up, without his arms and his cloak, by the attendants who were near and who ran to his aid. Even his javelin, which he was holding tightly in his hand, fell from his grasp and lay twenty feet or more away from him.

There were frequent earth-tremors in the palace at Aachen; and in the apartments where Charlemagne lived the wooden beams of the ceiling kept on creaking. The cathedral in which he was subse-quently buried was struck by lightning and the golden apple which adorned the highest point of the roof was dashed off by a thunderbolt and thrown on the top of the Bishop's house, which was next door. In the cathedral itself, along the edge of the horizontal ribs which ran right round the interior of the building and divided the upper arches from those on ground level, there was written in red ochre an inscrip-tion which recorded the name of the man who had constructed it. The words *Karolus Princeps* were included in the first phrase. In the very year of Charlemagne's death, only a few months before he died, people noticed that the lettering of the word *Princeps* was beginning to fade and that it eventually became illegible.

Charlemagne took no notice at all of these portents; or at least he refused to admit that any of them could have any connection with his own affairs.

---

* The bridge over the Rhine at Mainz was burned in May 813. As Einhard says, it was of wood, so that it could hardly have been expected to last for ever.

BOOK V

CHARLEMAGNE'S LAST WILL
AND TESTAMENT

Charlemagne resolved to draw up a will by which he could make
his daughters, and the sons whom his concubines had borne him,
heirs to some part of his property. He began this too late, however,
and it was never finished. Three years before his death he shared out
his treasures, his money, his clothes and his furniture, in the presence
of his friends and ministers. He instructed them to make absolutely
sure that the division which he had planned should be put into effect
after his death. He had a statement prepared to show just what he
wanted done with the objects which he had shared out.

The text of this document ran as follows:

In the name of the Lord God Almighty, the Father, the Son and
the Holy Ghost. This catalogue of his possessions and these sugges-
tions for their disposal have been drawn up by Charles, the august,
most pious and most glorious Lord and Emperor, in the eight
hundred and eleventh year after the Incarnation of our Lord Jesus
Christ, the forty-third year of Charlemagne's reign over the land of
the Franks, in the thirty-sixth year of his reign over Italy, in the
eleventh year of his being Emperor and in the fourth tax year.

With pious and prudent forethought he has resolved to make this
partition of his valuables and of the moneys which were stored up in
his treasure-house on that particular day, and with God's help he has
proceeded to do so. His essential objects in planning this division have
been to ensure that the distribution of alms which from long tradition
Christians offer from their personal effects should be made methodi-
cally and sensibly from his own fortune, too; and then that his heirs
should know clearly and without any possible misunderstanding
what ought to come to each of them and so should be able to divide
his possessions among themselves without lawsuit or dissension, each
receiving his allotted share.

With this intention and object in mind, he has first of all divided into three parts all the valuables and precious objects which were to be found in his treasure-house in the form of gold, silver, jewels and regalia on the day stipulated. The first third he has placed on one side. The remaining two thirds he has subdivided into twenty-one parts. This division of the two thirds into twenty-one parts has been made for the following reason. It is well known that there are twenty-one metropolitan cities in Charlemagne's kingdom. Each of these parts shall be handed by his heirs and friends to one of these cities to be used for charity. The Archbishop who at the time of Charlemagne's death is in charge of each of the sees in question shall receive the part allocated to his own diocese. He shall share it with his suffragans in the following way: one third shall go to his own church and the remaining two thirds shall be divided among the suffragans. Each of these subdivisions, which have been made from the aforesaid two thirds, according to the recognized number of twenty-one metro-politan cities, lies in its own coffer, separated systematically from the others and with the name of the city to which it is destined written clearly on it. The names of the metropolitan cities to which these alms or *eleemosyna* are to go are as follows: Rome, Ravenna, Milan, Cividale, Grado, Cologne, Mainz, Juvavum or Salzburg, Trier, Sens, Besançon, Lyons, Rouen, Rheims, Arles, Vienne, Moutiers-en-Tarantaise, Embrun, Bordeaux, Tours and Bourges.

The following use shall be made of the third which Charlemagne has decided to keep intact. When the other two thirds have been divided up in the way stated and have been stored away under seal, the remaining third, which has not been alienated from his personal possession by any bond, shall be used for day-to-day expenses. It shall be so used as long as he remains alive or judges that he still has need of it. After his death or his voluntary withdrawal from the affairs of this world it shall be split up into four subdivisions. One of these quarters shall be added to the twenty-one shares already men-tioned. The second quarter, destined for his own sons and daughters, and for the sons and daughters of his sons shall be divided between them in a just and reasonable manner. The third quarter shall be devoted to the use of the poor, as is the custom among Christians. In the same way, the fourth quarter shall be shared out and shall come as a pension, in the name of Christian charity, to the servants, both men and women, who perform their duties in the royal palace.

Charlemagne has decreed that to this third part of his total fortune which like the other two thirds, is composed of gold and silver, shall be added all the vessels and utensils of bronze, iron and other metals, together with his arms, clothes and all other movable objects, whether of value or not, and for whatsoever use they are put, such as curtains, bedcovers, tapestries, woollen stuffs, skins, harnesses, and all else which happened to be found in his treasure-house and his wardrobe on that particular day, so that the subdivisions of that third part may be larger and the distribution of alms find its way to a greater number of people.

He has ordered that his chapel, that is to say the furnishings of his church, including both what he has himself given and collected together and what has come to him by inheritance from his father, should remain intact and should not be split up in any way. If, however, any vessels, books or other equipment are found there which have most clearly not been given by him to the chapel, then these may be purchased and owned by anyone who wishes to have them, providing that they pay a reasonable price. In the same way he has decreed that the great collection of books which he has made in his library shall be bought at a reasonable price by anybody who wants to have them, and the money given to the poor.

Among his other treasures and property there are three tables made of silver and a particularly big and heavy one made of gold. He has made the following decisions and decrees about these. The first table, which is square in shape and on which is traced a map of the city of Constantinople, shall be sent to Rome to the cathedral of the blessed Apostle Peter, along with the other gifts which are set aside for that purpose. The second table, which is circular, and which is engraved with a map of the city of Rome, shall be dispatched to the bishopric of the church of Ravenna. The third, which is far superior to the others, both in the beauty of its workmanship and in weight, and on which is engraved in fine and delicate tracery a design which shows the entire universe in three concentric circles, shall be added to that third part which is to be divided among his heirs and those who receive alms. With it shall go the golden table, which is listed as the fourth one.

Charlemagne has drawn up this catalogue and partition of his goods in the presence of the following bishops, abbots and counts who were able to attend. Their names are set out in the following list:

Bishops: Hildebald, Richolf, Arn, Wolfar, Bernoin, Laidrad, John, Theodulf, Jesse, Heito, Waltgaud.
Abbots: Fridugis, Adalung, Engilbert, Irmino.
Counts: Walah, Meginher, Otulf, Stephen, Unruoc, Burchard, Meginhard, Hatto, Rihwin, Edo, Ercangar, Gerold, Bero, Hildigern, Hroccolf.

Charlemagne's son Lewis, who succeeded him by divine right, read this statement and acted upon it with complete scrupulousness as soon as he possibly could after his father's death.

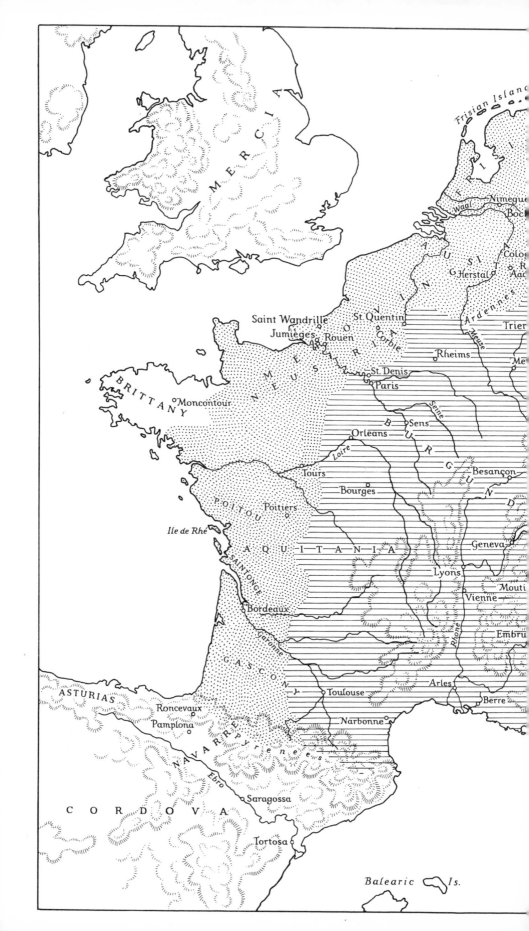

MERCIA

Frisian Islands

F R I S I

Waal Nimeguen
Boc

A U S T R A S I A

Colo
Aac

Herstal

Ardennes

Saint Wandrille St. Quentin Trier
Jumièges Rouen Corbie Me

N E U S T R I A Rheims

St. Denis
Paris

BRITTANY Moncontour B U R Sens
Senne

Orleans G U N
Loire

Tours Besançon

Bourges D

POITOU Poitiers

Ile de Rhé Geneva

A Q U I T A N I A

SAINTONGE Lyons

Mouti
Vienne

Bordeaux

Garonne Embru
Rhone

G A S C O N Y Arles

ASTURIAS Toulouse Berre

Roncevaux

Pamplona Narbonne

N A V A R R E Pyrenees

Ebro

C O R D O V A Saragossa

Tortosa

Balearic Is.

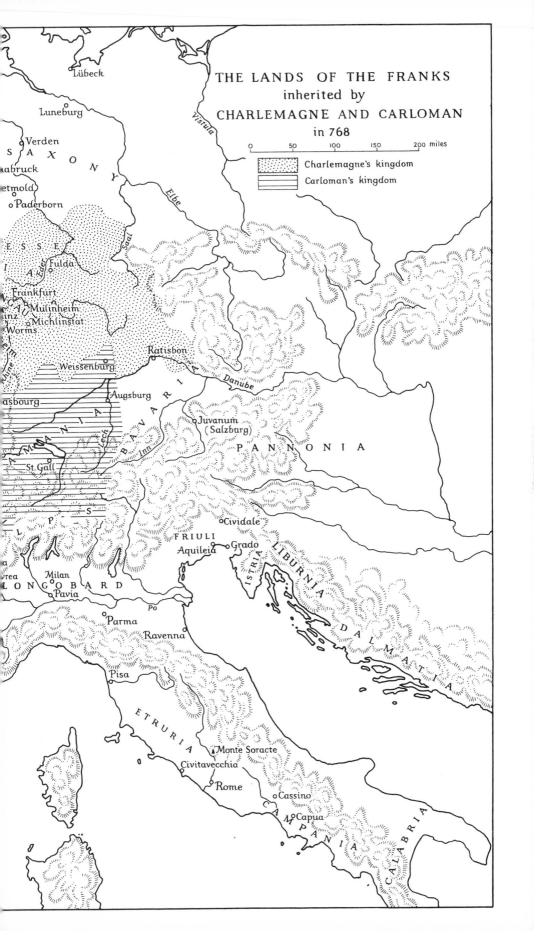

THE LANDS OF THE FRANKS
inherited by
CHARLEMAGNE AND CARLOMAN
in 768

0   50   100   150   200 miles

Charlemagne's kingdom
Carloman's kingdom

Lübeck

Luneburg

Verden

SAXONY

abruck

etmold

Paderborn

ESS

Fulda

Frankfurt

Mulinheim

inz   Michlinstat

Worms

Weissenburg

Ratisbon

asbourg

Augsburg

Danube

St. Gall

MANIA

BAVARIA

Lech

Inn

Juvanum
(Salzburg)

PANNONIA

Cividale

FRIULI

Aquileia   Grado

ISTRIA

LIBURNIA

rea

Milan

LONGOBARD

Pavia

Po

Parma

Ravenna

DALMATIA

Pisa

ETRURIA

Monte Soracte

Civitavecchia

Rome

Cassino

CAMPANIA

Capua

CALABRIA

Vistula

Elbe

Saal

Verden

SAXONY

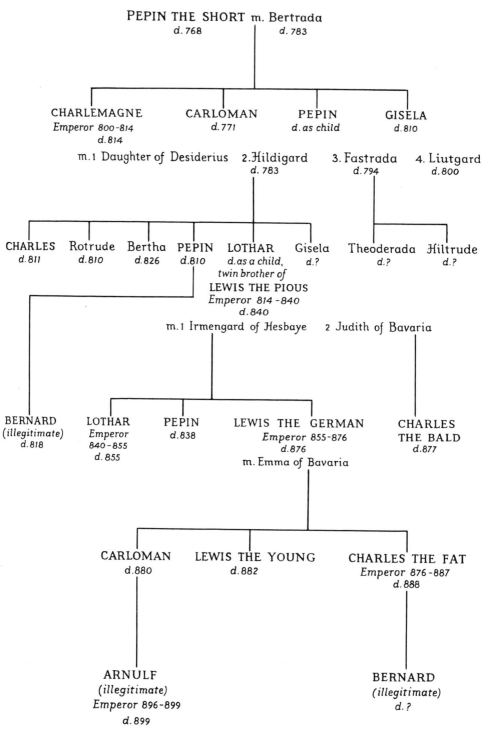

PEPIN THE SHORT m. Bertrada
d. 768   d. 783

CHARLEMAGNE   CARLOMAN   PEPIN   GISELA
Emperor 800-814   d. 771   d. as child   d. 810
d. 814

m. 1 Daughter of Desiderius   2. Hildigard   3. Fastrada   4. Liutgard
d. 783   d. 794   d. 800

CHARLES   Rotrude   Bertha   PEPIN   LOTHAR   Gisela   Theoderada   Hiltrude
d. 811   d. 810   d. 826   d. 810   d. as a child,   d. ?   d. ?   d. ?
                                      twin brother of
                                      LEWIS THE PIOUS
                                      Emperor 814-840
                                      d. 840

m. 1 Irmengard of Hesbaye   2 Judith of Bavaria

BERNARD   LOTHAR   PEPIN   LEWIS THE GERMAN   CHARLES
(illegitimate)   Emperor   d. 838   Emperor 855-876   THE BALD
d. 818   840-855   d. 876   d. 877
              d. 855
                                      m. Emma of Bavaria

CARLOMAN   LEWIS THE YOUNG   CHARLES THE FAT
d. 880   d. 882   Emperor 876-887
                                      d. 888

ARNULF   BERNARD
(illegitimate)   (illegitimate)
Emperor 896-899   d. ?
d. 899

GENEALOGY OF THE CAROLINGIANS

SOURCES OF ILLUSTRATIONS

Ninth-century equestrian bronze statuette reputedly of Charlemagne but possibly Charles the Bald. The horse is fifteenth-century. Paris, Louvre.

The coronation of Charlemagne. Charlemagne enthroned. *Chroniques de Saint Denis.* Paris, Bibl. Ste Gen., MS.782, fº 121vº.

The coronation of Charlemagne as Emperor in Saint Peter's, Rome, by Pope Leo III on 25 December 800. *Chronique de Bauduin d'Avesnes.* Paris, Bibl. de l'Ars., MS.5089, fº 162v., (1462).

Archbishop Turpin and Einhard reading the books which they have written about Charlemagne. *Grandes Chroniques de France.* Brussels, Bibl. Roy., MS.3, fº 109v., (early 15th century).

Edwin, monk of Christchurch, Canterbury, copying a manuscript. (Probably a self-portrait.) Camb., Trin. Coll., MS.R.17.1, fº 283r. (*c.* 1148–49).

A page of a library catalogue copied *c.* 800. Oxf., Bod. Libr., MS.Laud Misc. 126, fº 260r.

Monks singing in their stalls. Brit. Mus., MS Cotton, Dom. A. XVII, fº 122v. (*c.* 1430).

Charlemagne and his troops set off for Spain. The veterans from Spain return to Aachen. *Liber Sancti Jacobi.* Saint Jacques de Compostella, Arch. cat. MS. Calixtinus, fº 162v. (late 12th century).

Charlemagne in his tent at the siege of Pamplona. *L'Entrée en Espagne.* Venice, Bibl. Marc., MS. Fr. XXI, fº 136v. (*c.* 1350).

The battle of Roncevaux. *Grandes Chroniques de France.* Paris, Bibl. Nat., MS. Rés. vélin, 725, (1493).

Foreign envoys bring a message to Charlemagne. *L'Entrée en Espagne.* Venice, Bibl. Marc., MS. Fr. XXI, f⁰ 8r. (*c.* 1350).

Lewis the Pious, son of Charlemagne. Rome, Vat. Libr., MS. Reg. Lat. 124, f⁰ 4v. (9th century).

Charlemagne with his sister Gisela and Saint Giles. *Psautier de Lambert le Bègue.* Liège, Bibl. Univ., MS. 431, f⁰ 96v. (1255–60).

A sword which is supposed to have belonged to Charlemagne. Paris, Louvre.

Saint Augustine of Hippo, as imagined by a twelfth-century miniaturist of Saint Augustine's Abbey, Canterbury. *De Civitate Dei.* Florence, Bibl. Laur., MS., Plut. XII.17, f⁰ 3v. (early 12th century).

The Molsheim brooch. Darmstadt, Hess. Landesmus (8th century).

A reliquary which is supposed to have belonged to the Saxon Widukind in the late eighth century. Berlin, Staatl. Mus.

The publishers would like to thank the owners of the original material listed above for permission to reproduce in this book.

The cipher of Charlemagne used on the binding and endpapers is taken from a document dated 774.

The map and genealogy were drawn by K. C. Jordan F.R.G.S.